DISCOVER
The Nervous and Digestive Systems

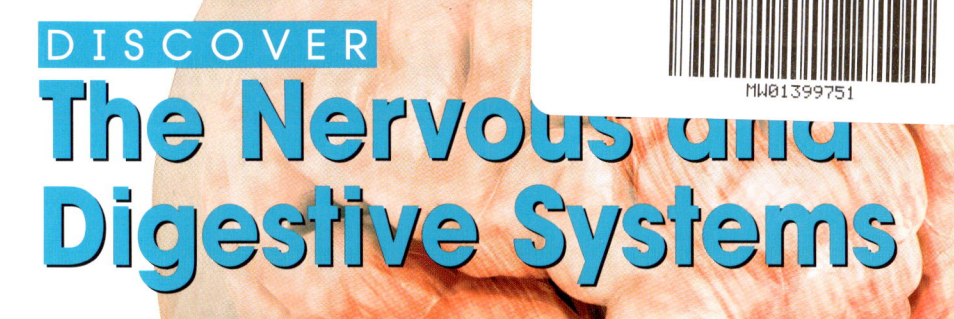

by Barbara Andrews

Table of Contents

Introduction 2
Chapter 1 What Does the Nervous System Control?... 4
Chapter 2 How Does the Digestive System Help People?............ 10
Chapter 3 What Does the Human Body Have?...... 14
Conclusion 18
Concept Map 20
Glossary 22
Index 24

Introduction

The **human body** has many body systems. The human body has a **nervous system**. The human body has a **digestive system**.

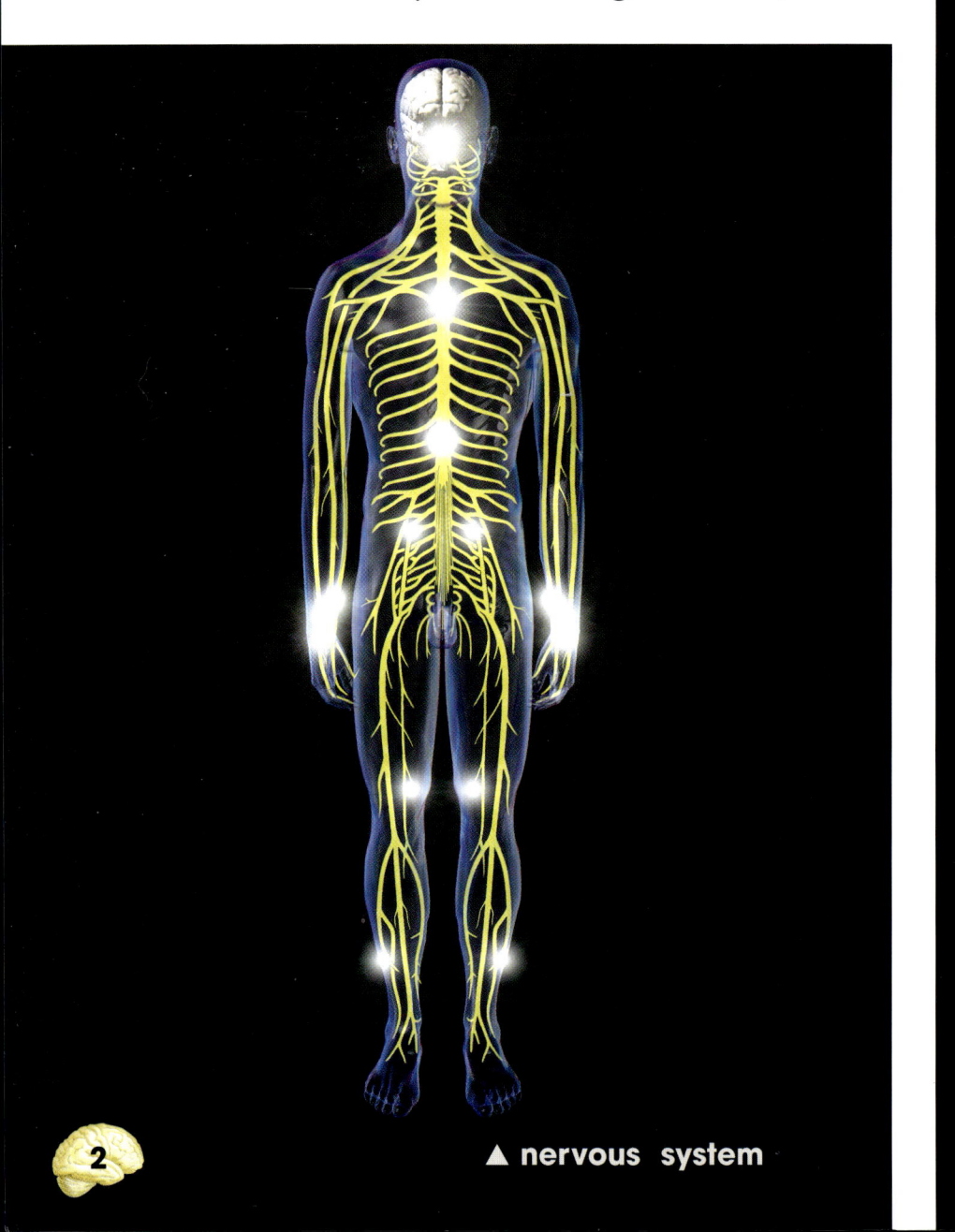

▲ nervous system

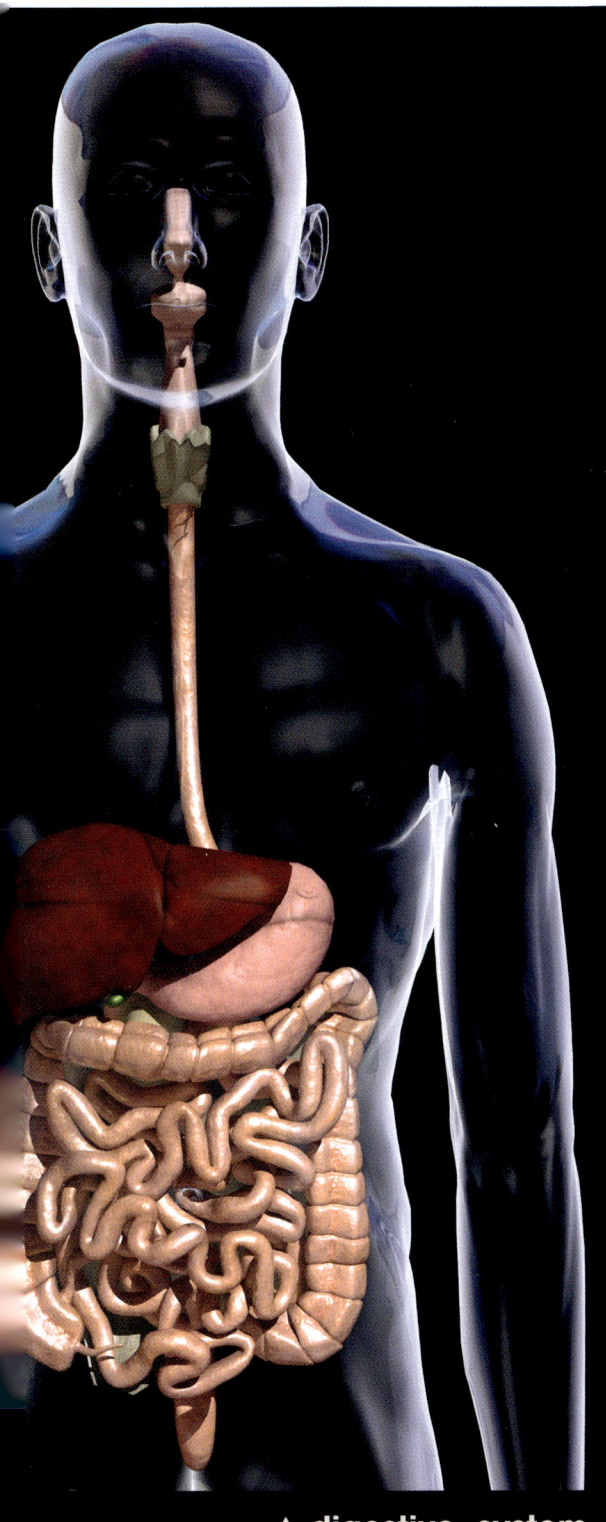

Words to Know

brain

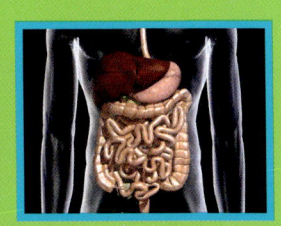

digestive system

human body

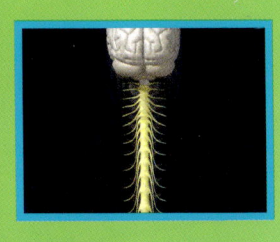

nerves

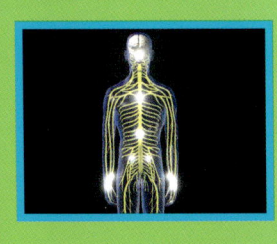

nervous system

stomach

▲ digestive system

See the Glossary on page 22.

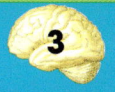

3

Chapter 1

What Does the Nervous System Control?

The nervous system controls all body systems.

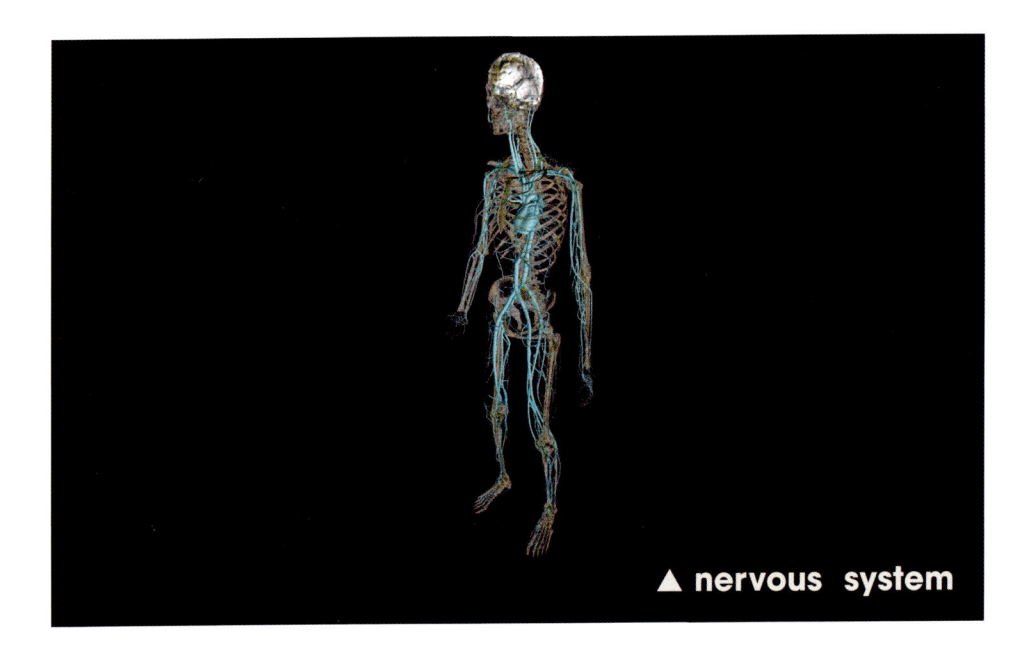

▲ nervous system

The nervous system controls thinking.

I will move the queen.

▲ People think because of the nervous system.

The nervous system controls decisions.

Grey or gold?

▲ People decide because of the nervous system.

5

Chapter 1

The nervous system controls hearing.

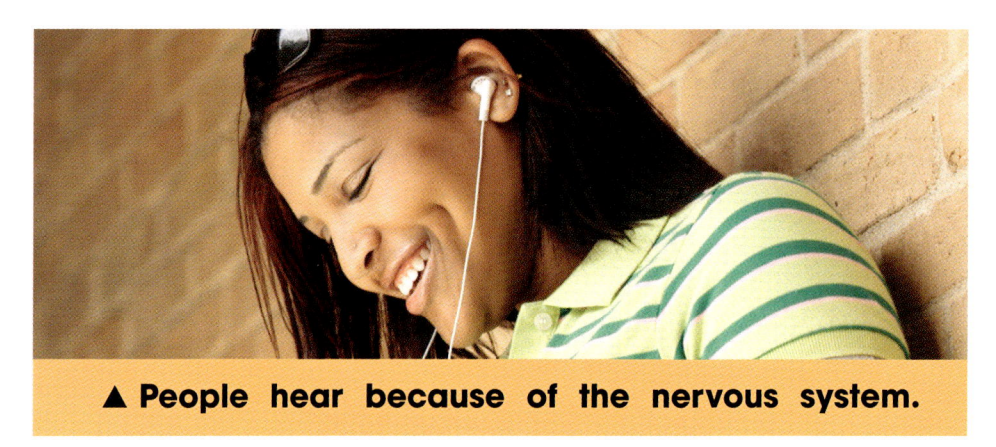

▲ People hear because of the nervous system.

The nervous system controls seeing.

▲ People see because of the nervous system.

It's a Fact

People have five senses:

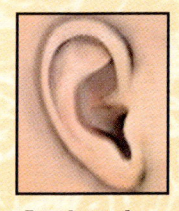

1. hearing    2. sight 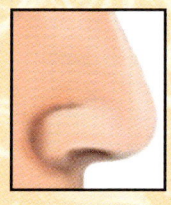   3. smell 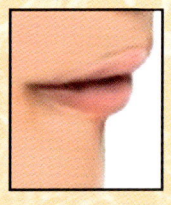   4. taste    5. touch

What Does the Nervous System Control?

The nervous system controls smelling.

▲ People smell because of the nervous system.

The nervous system controls tasting.

▲ People taste because of the nervous system.

The nervous system controls feeling.

▲ People feel because of the nervous system.

Chapter 1

The nervous system controls learning. The nervous system controls reading.

▲ People learn because of the nervous system.

The nervous system controls writing.

▲ People write because of the nervous system.

What Does the Nervous System Control?

The nervous system controls memory.

▲ People remember because of the nervous system.

Chapter 2

How Does the Digestive System Help People?

The digestive system helps people get hungry.

▲ The human body gets hungry.

The digestive system helps people use food.

▲ The human body uses food.

11

Chapter 2

The digestive system helps people get nutrients.

▲ The human body gets nutrients.

Did You Know?
Healthy foods have many nutrients.

How Does the Digestive System Help People?

The digestive system helps people get energy.

▲ The human body gets energy.

The digestive system helps people stay healthy.

▲ The human body stays healthy.

13

Chapter 3

What Does the Human Body Have?

The human body has a **brain**. The human body has a brain stem.

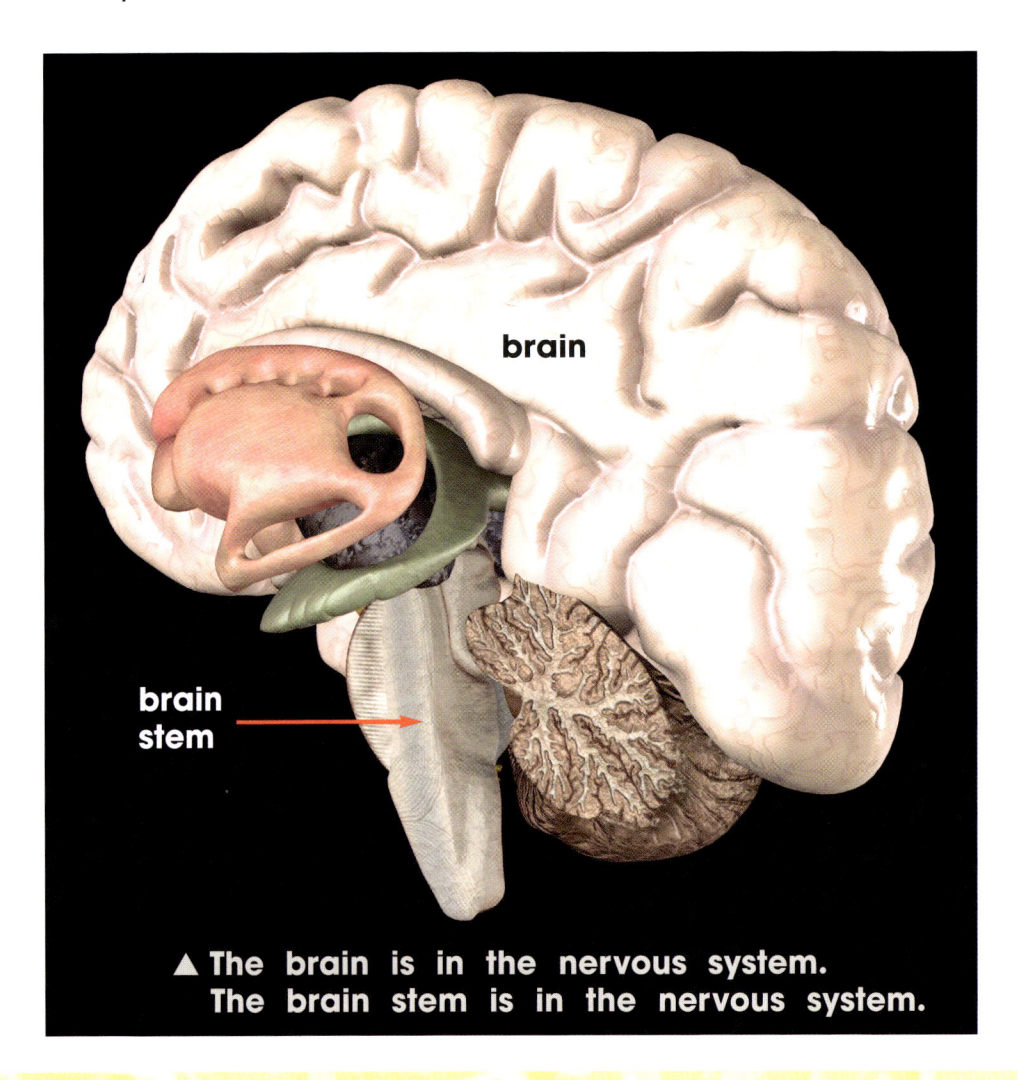

brain

brain stem

▲ The brain is in the nervous system. The brain stem is in the nervous system.

Did You Know?

The brain controls the nervous system. The brain controls the human body.

14

The human body has a spinal cord. The human body has **nerves**.

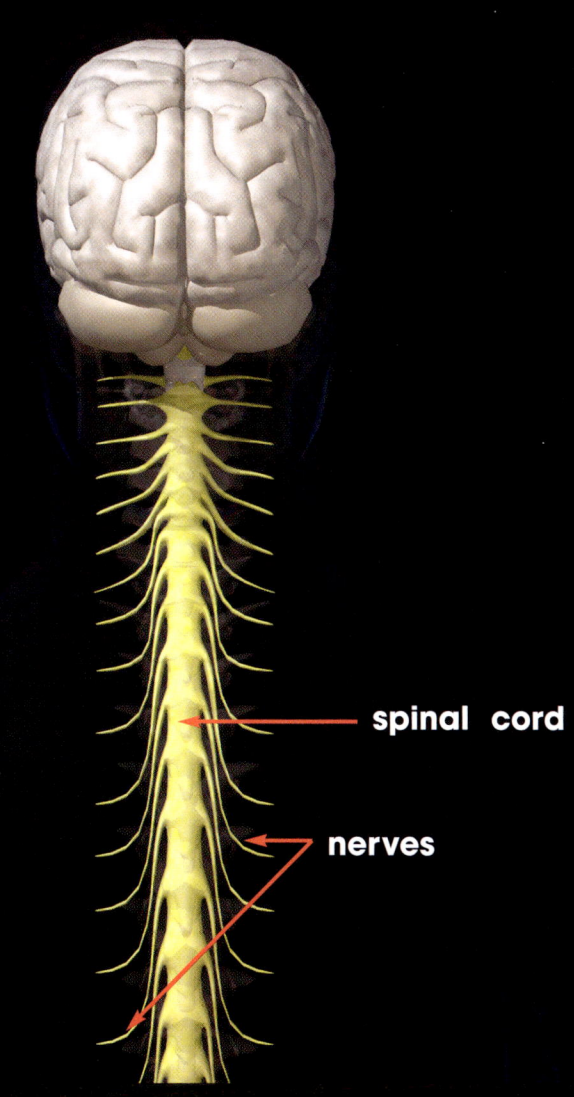

spinal cord

nerves

▲ The spinal cord is in the nervous system. Nerves are in the nervous system.

Chapter 3

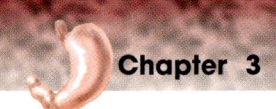

The human body has a mouth.

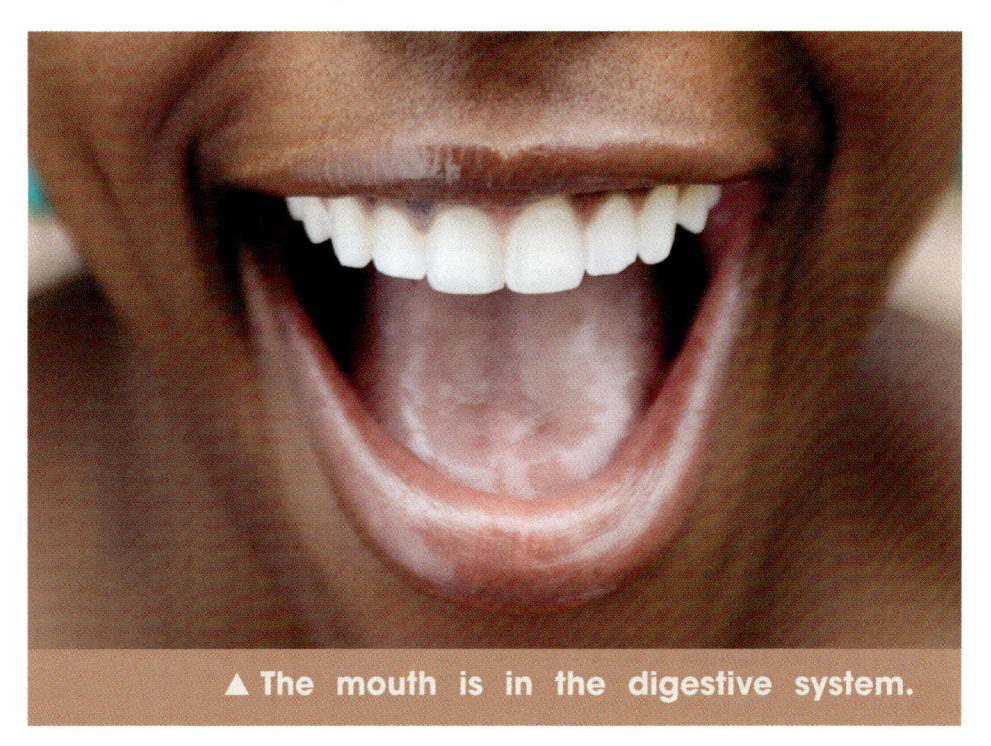

▲ The mouth is in the digestive system.

The human body has saliva.

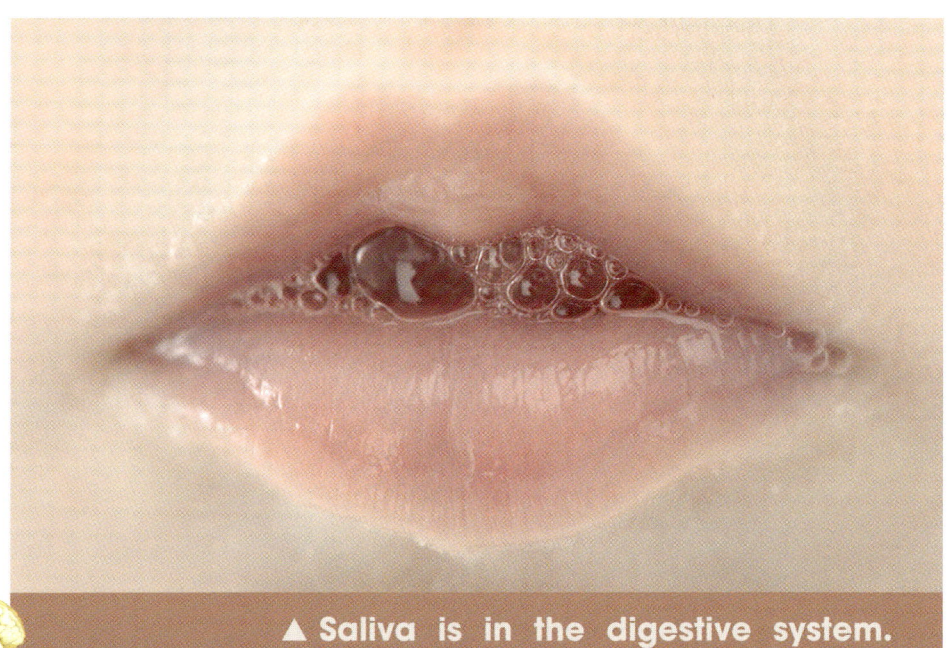

▲ Saliva is in the digestive system.

What Does the Human Body Have?

The human body has an esophagus.
The human body has a **stomach**.

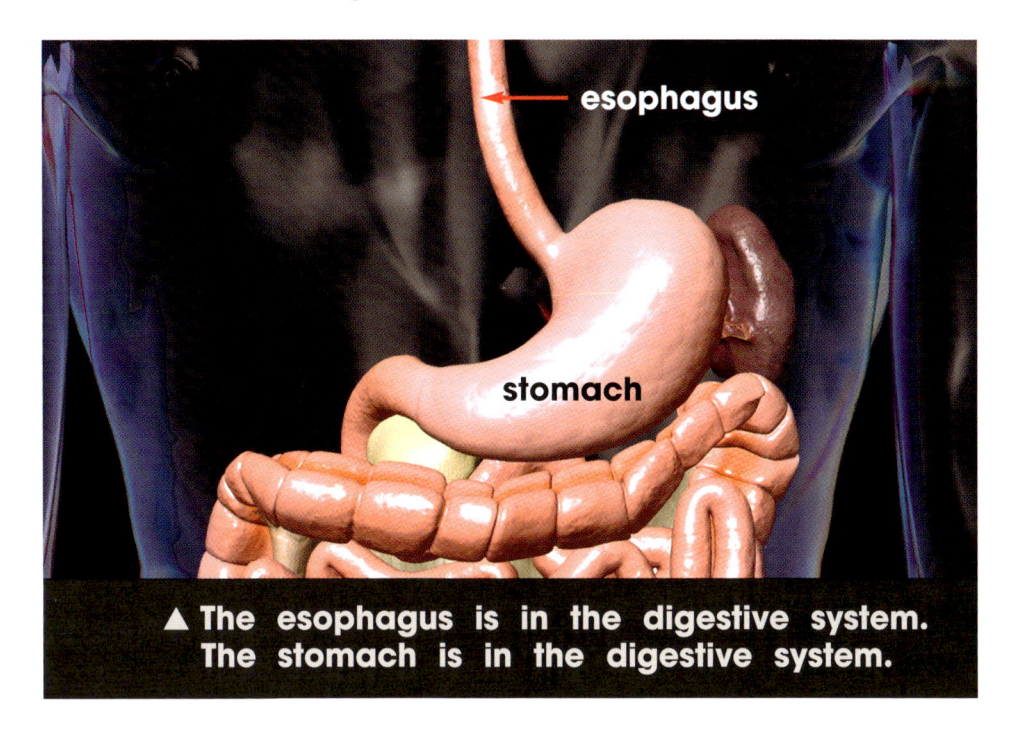

▲ The esophagus is in the digestive system.
The stomach is in the digestive system.

The human body has intestines.

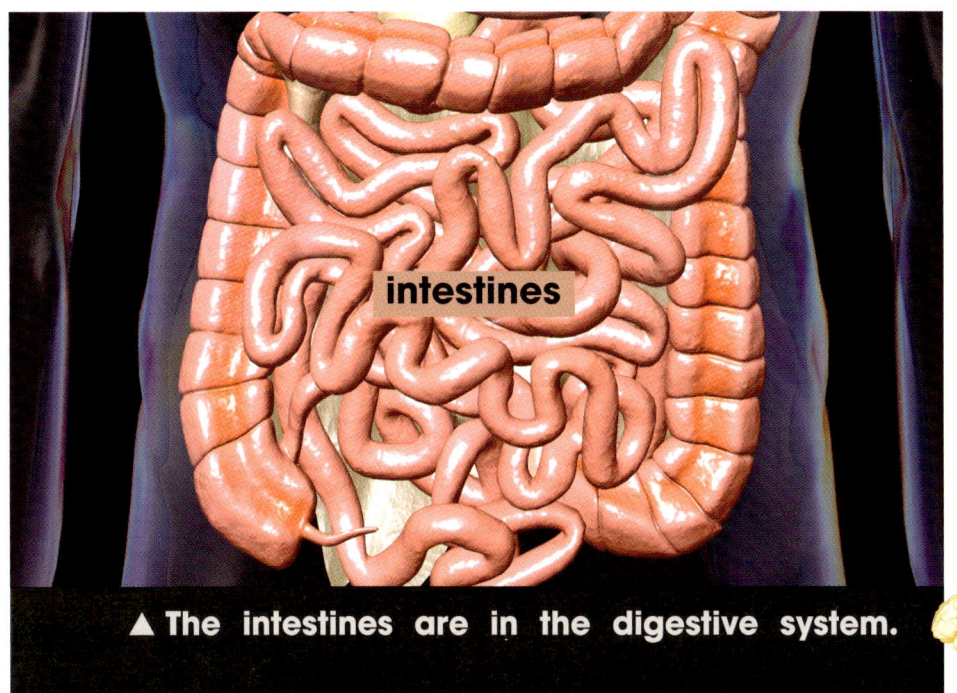

▲ The intestines are in the digestive system.

Conclusion

The body has systems. The body has a nervous system. The body has a digestive system.

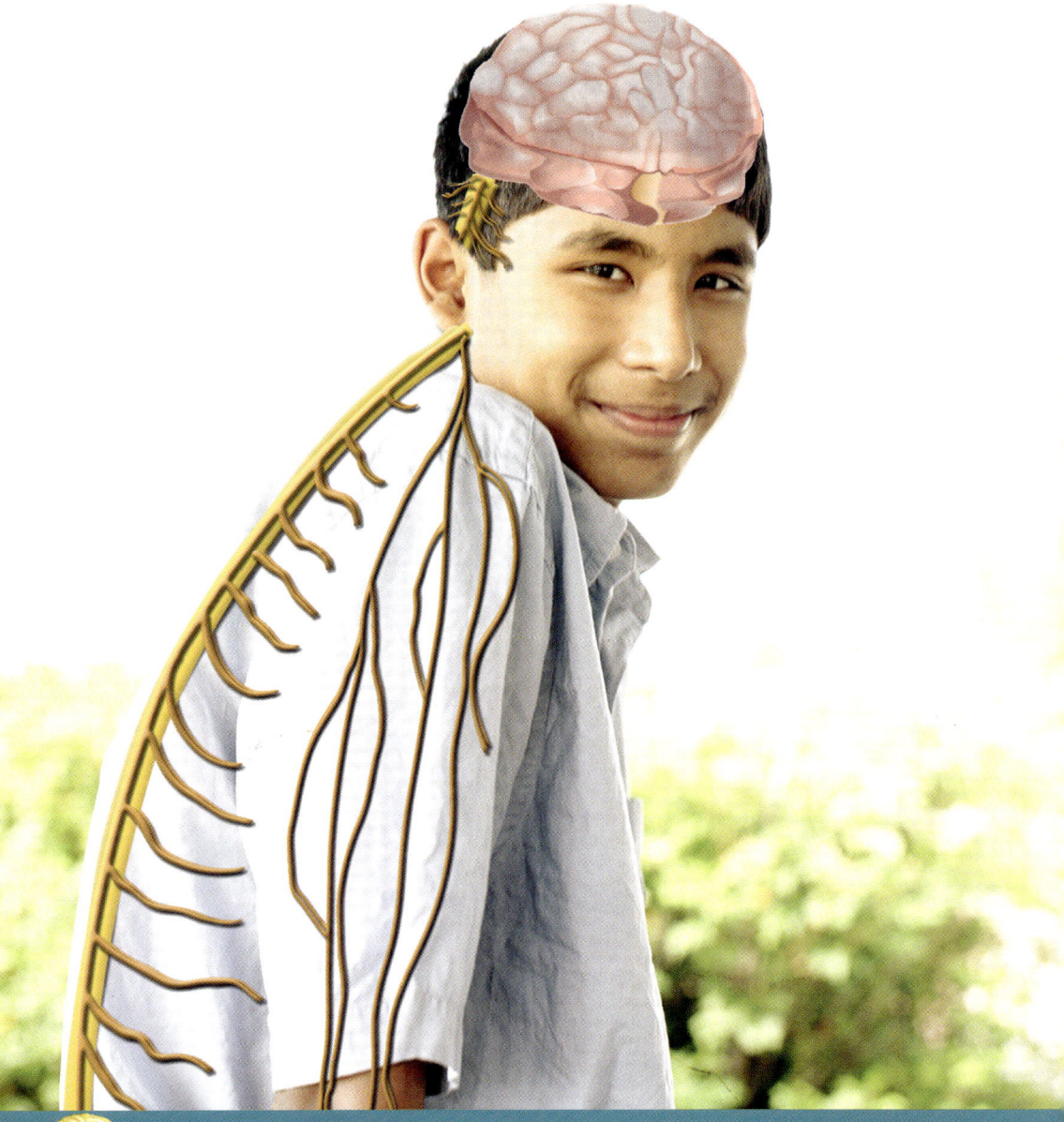

▲ The nervous system has parts.

▲ The digestive system has parts.

19

Concept Map

The Nervous and Digestive Systems

What Does the Nervous System Control?

- all body systems
- thinking
- decisions
- hearing
- seeing
- smelling
- tasting
- feeling
- learning
- reading
- writing
- memory

How Does the Digestive System Help People?

- feel hungry
- use food
- get nutrients
- get energy
- stay healthy

What Does the Human Body Have?

brain
brain stem
nerves
mouth
saliva
esophagus
stomach
intestines

Glossary

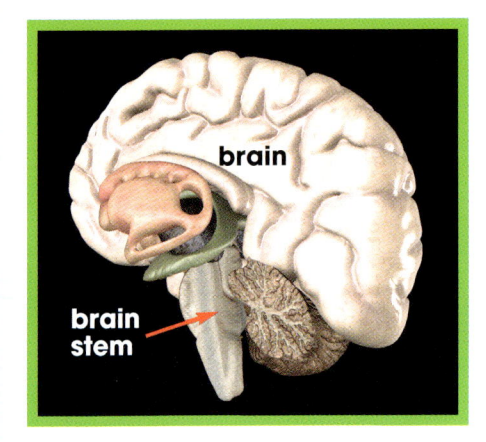

brain part of the nervous system that has thoughts

*The human body has a **brain**.*

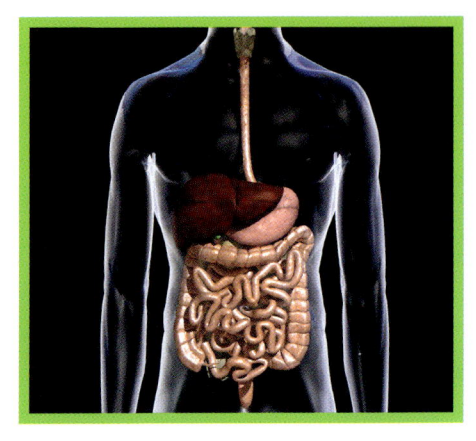

digestive system body system that prepares food for the body to use

*The **digestive system** helps people get nutrients.*

human body all parts of a person

*The **human body** has many body systems.*

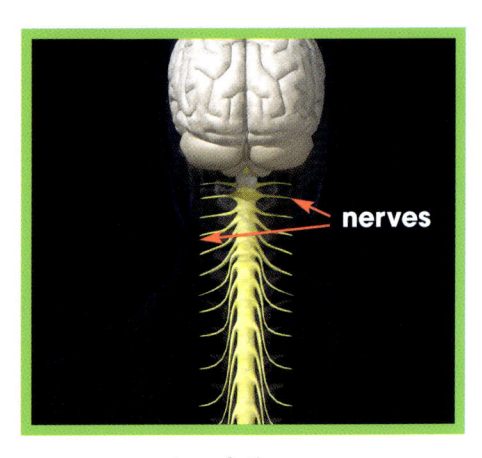

nerves parts of the nervous system that carry messages

*The human body has **nerves**.*

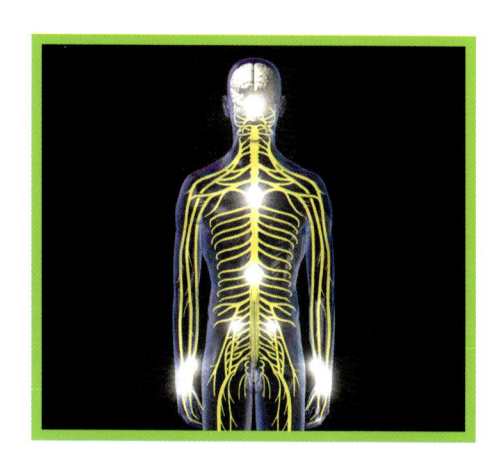

nervous system body system that controls all other systems

*The **nervous system** controls hearing.*

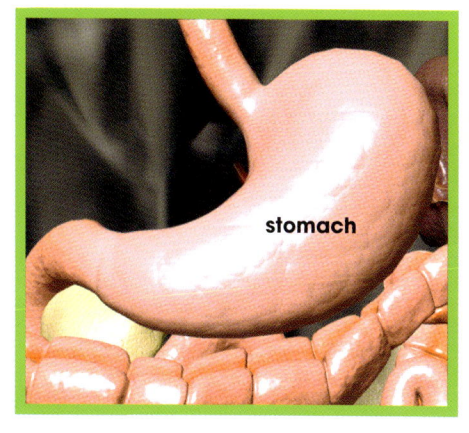

stomach body part that is between the esophagus and intestines

*The human body has a **stomach**.*

Index

brain, 14

brain stem, 14

digestive system, 2, 10–13, 18

energy, 13

esophagus, 17

human body, 2, 14–17

intestines, 17

mouth, 16

nerves, 15

nervous system, 2, 4–9, 18

nutrients, 12

saliva, 16

spinal cord, 15

stomach, 17

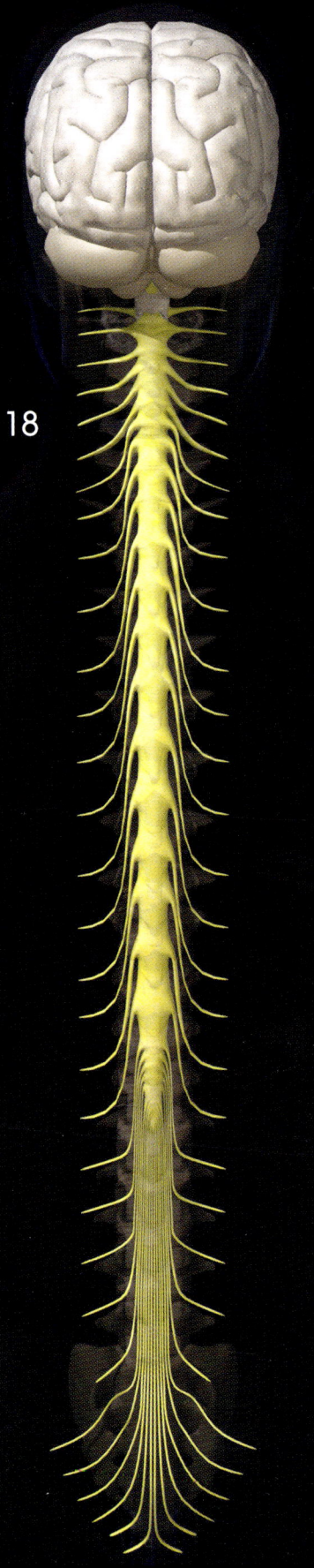